ELMHURST PUBLIC LIBRARY

3 1135 01980 6675

W9-BNL-096

J
945
Mar

Italy

by Joyce Markovics

Consultant: Karla Ruiz, MA
Teachers College, Columbia University
New York, New York

BEARPORT
PUBLISHING

New York, New York

ELMHURST PUBLIC LIBRARY
125 S. Prospect Avenue
Elmhurst, IL 60126-3298

Credits

Cover, © Koraysa/iStock and © Fedor Selivanov/Shutterstock; TOC, © Warut Prathaksithorn/Shutterstock; 4, © Mario Savoia/Shutterstock; 5L, © Fedor Selivanov/Shutterstock; 5R, © Noam Armonn/Shutterstock; 7, © JeniFoto/Shutterstock; 8, © macumazahn/Shutterstock; 9, © mkistryn/iStock; 10T, © shahreen/Shutterstock; 10B, © GlobalP/iStock; 11, © tomazl/iStock; 11B, © Dmitri Gristsenko/Shutterstock; 12, © Styve Reineck/Shutterstock; 13, © andersphoto/Shutterstock; 14–15, © Ugis Riba/Shutterstock; 15T, © r.nagy/Shutterstock; 16, © S.Borisov/Shutterstock; 17, © Noppasin/Shutterstock; 18, © Alliance/Shutterstock; 19, © Cultura Creative (RF)/Alamy; 20, © tzahiV/iStock; 21, © PhotoEd/Shutterstock; 22–23, © David Levenson/Alamy; 24–25, © Paolo Bona/Shutterstock; 25T, © Juri Pozzi/Shutterstock; 25B, © Dennis van de Water/Shutterstock; 26T, © photogolfer/Shutterstock; 26B, © Didier ZYLBERYNG/Alamy; 27L, © Tony Baggett/Shutterstock; 27R, Public Domain; 28, © ArtMarie/iStock; 29, © Stuart Black/Alamy; 30T, © Viktor Kunz/Shutterstock and © spinetta/Shutterstock; 30B, © Antonio Gravante/Shutterstock; 31 (T to B), © S-F/Shutterstock, © pcruciatti/Shutterstock, © S.Borisov/Shutterstock, © Rudy Balasko/Shutterstock, © George Clerk/iStock, and © ronnybas/Shutterstock; 32, © Vitaly Raduntsev/Shutterstock.

Publisher: Kenn Goin
Senior Editor: Joyce Tavolacci
Creative Director: Spencer Brinker
Design: Debrah Kaiser
Photo Researcher: Thomas Persano

Library of Congress Cataloging-in-Publication Data

Names: Markovics, Joyce L., author.
Title: Italy / by Joyce Markovics.
Other titles: Countries we come from.
Description: New York, New York : Bearport Publishing, [2017] | Series: Countries we come from | Audience: Ages 5–8. | Includes bibliographical references and index.
Identifiers: LCCN 2016037729 (print) | LCCN 2016039904 (ebook) | ISBN 9781684020584 (library) | ISBN 9781684021109 (ebook)
Subjects: LCSH: Italy—Juvenile literature. | Italy—History—Juvenile literature.
Classification: LCC DG417 .M354 2017 (print) | LCC DG417 (ebook) | DDC 945—dc23
LC record available at https://lccn.loc.gov/2016037729

Copyright © 2017 Bearport Publishing Company, Inc. All rights reserved. No part of this publication may be reproduced in whole or in part, stored in any retrieval system, or transmitted in any form or by any means, electronic, mechanical, photocopying, recording, or otherwise, without written permission from the publisher.

For more information, write to Bearport Publishing Company, Inc., 45 West 21st Street, Suite 3B, New York, New York 10010. Printed in the United States of America.

10 9 8 7 6 5 4 3 2 1

Contents

Spectacular

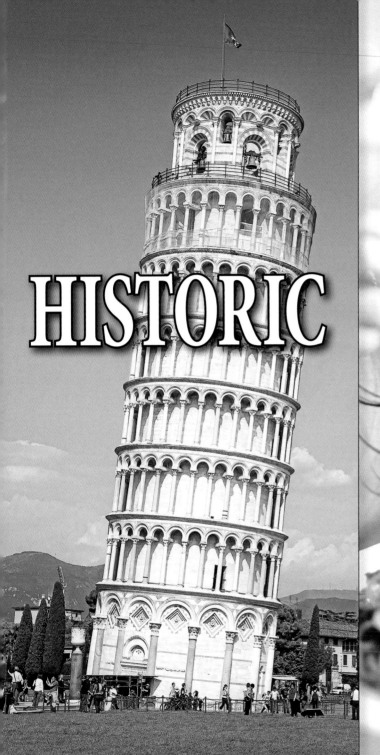

HISTORIC

Delicious

5

Italy is a country in southern Europe.

It's shaped like a boot!

Water surrounds the country
on three sides.

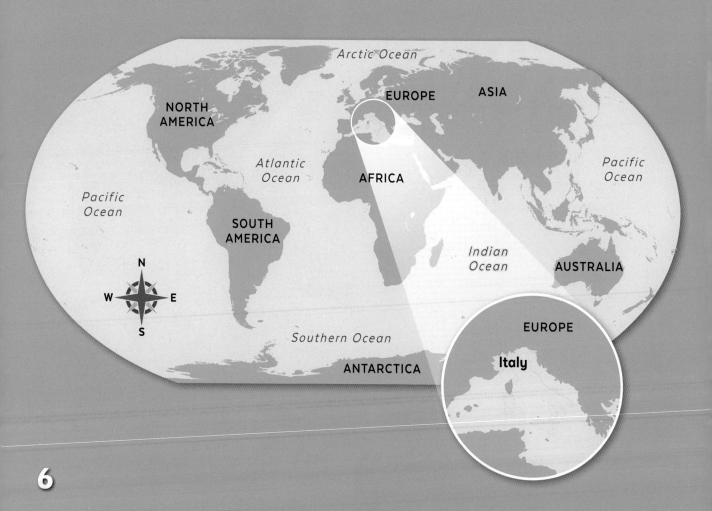

More than 60 million people live in Italy.

Italy is known for its beautiful landscapes.

There are tall, **majestic** mountains.

Italy's tallest mountain—
Monte Bianco—rises more
than 15,700 feet (4,785 m)!

There are also thick forests and flat, dry plains.

Much of Italy's land is used for farming.

People grow tomatoes, olives, and grapes.

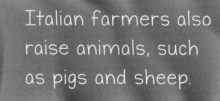

Italian farmers also raise animals, such as pigs and sheep.

10

grapevines

The grapes are used to make wine.

Italy has a very long history.

People have lived there for thousands of years.

Augustus, a famous Roman ruler

One group—the Romans—ruled for 400 years.

They built **vast** towns and cities.

Before the Romans, the Greeks and Etruscans ruled Italy.

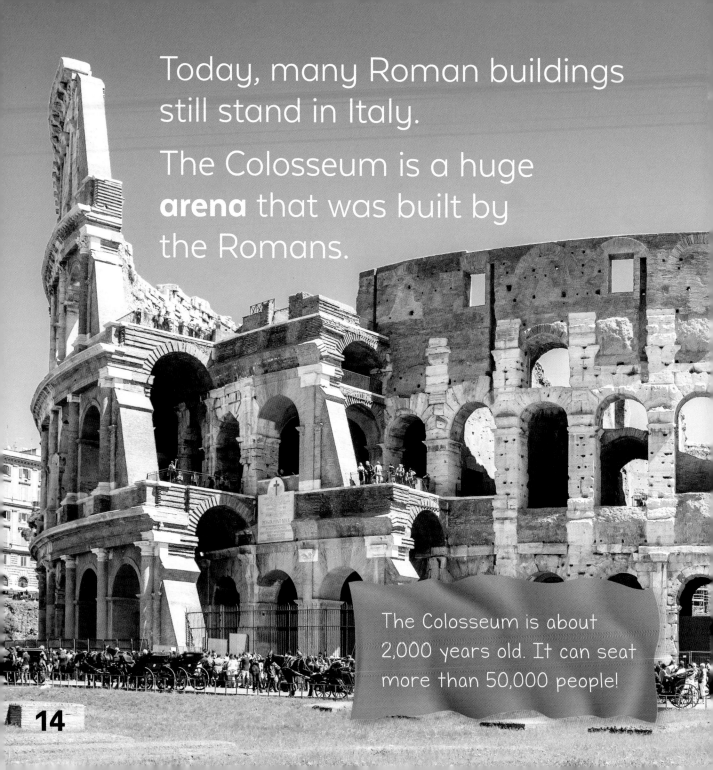

Today, many Roman buildings still stand in Italy.

The Colosseum is a huge **arena** that was built by the Romans.

The Colosseum is about 2,000 years old. It can seat more than 50,000 people!

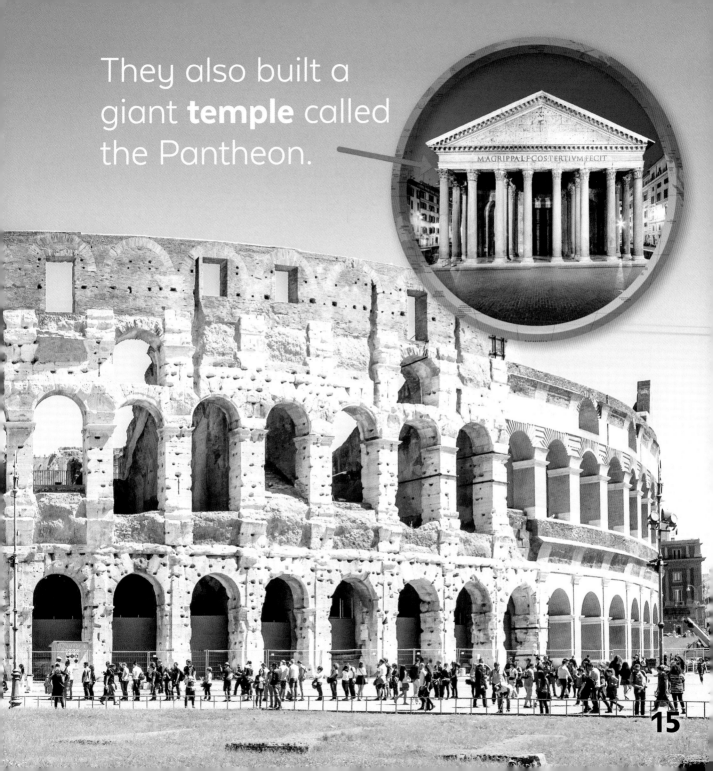

They also built a giant **temple** called the Pantheon.

MAGRIPPA·L·F·COSTERTIVM·FECIT

Rome is the **capital** of Italy.

It's also the country's largest city.

More than 2.8 million people live there.

a church
in Milan

Milan is Italy's
second-largest city.

The main language in Italy is Italian.

This is how you say *hi* and *bye* in Italian:

Ciao (CHOW)

Italian is based on an **ancient** language called Latin.

18

This is how you say *I'm hungry:*

Ho fame (OH FAH-may)

19

Italy is famous for its flavorful food.
Pasta and risotto (ri-ZOH-toh) are
two favorites.

There are more than 600 shapes of pasta!

Risotto is made with cooked rice and broth. Yum!

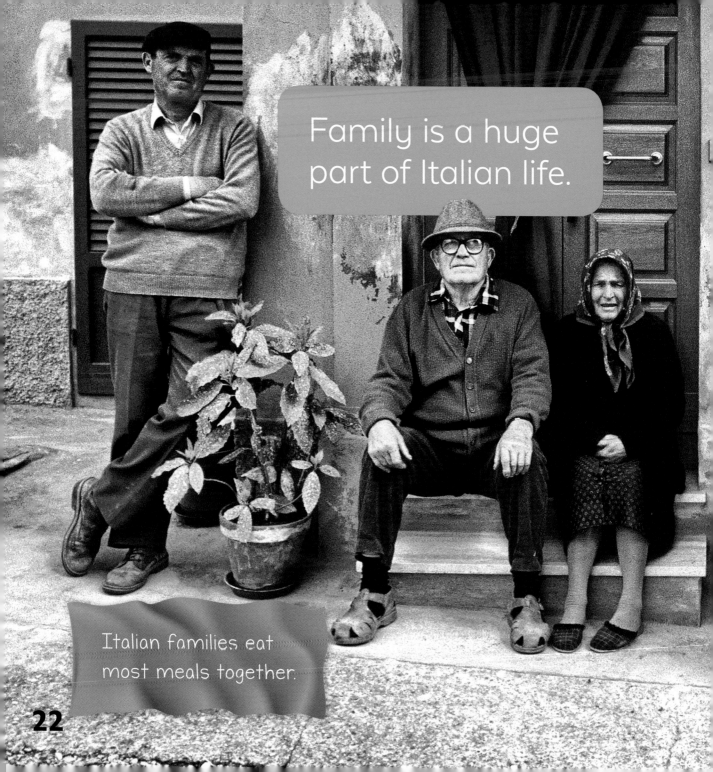

Family is a huge part of Italian life.

Italian families eat most meals together.

Adult children often live with their parents.

Grandparents live with the family, too!

23

Italians love soccer. More than 80,000 fans pack into San Siro Stadium in Milan.

When the teams score, fans go wild!

What other sports do Italians enjoy? People like skiing and snowboarding in the mountains!

Italy is known for its amazing art.

Churches overflow with paintings and sculptures.

People can also see art at Italy's many museums.

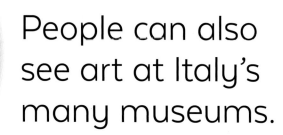

a statue by Michelangelo

Michelangelo and Leonardo da Vinci are two famous Italian artists.

a painting by Leonardo

More than 50 million people visit Italy each year.

It's the fifth most visited country in the world!

the volcano that almost destroyed Pompeii

Pompeii (pom-PEY) is a popular place to visit. It's an ancient town that was nearly destroyed by a volcano about 2,000 years ago!

Fast Facts

Capital city: Rome

Population of Italy: More than 60 million

Main language: Italian

Money: Euro

Major religion: Roman Catholic

Neighboring countries: Switzerland, Slovenia, France, and Austria

Cool Fact: Pizza was invented in Naples, Italy.

ancient (AYN-shunt) very old

arena (uh-REE-nuh) a large building where sporting events are held

capital (KAP-uh-tuhl) a city where a country's government is based

majestic (*muh*-JES-tik) grand

temple (TEM-puhl) a building used for worship

vast (VAST) huge in size, area, or amount

Index

Read More

Borlenghi, Patricia. *Find Out About Italy.* Hauppauge, NY: Barron's (2006).

Simmons, Walter. *Italy (Blastoff! Readers: Exploring Countries).* Minnetonka, MN: Bellwether (2010).

Learn More Online

To learn more about Italy, visit **www.bearportpublishing.com/CountriesWeComeFrom**

About the Author

Joyce Markovics lives along the Hudson River in a very old house. Part of her family hails from Sicily, a large island off the southern tip of Italy.